My Family Tree

Written by Mike Lefroy

Illustrated by Deborah Baldassi

ETA Cuisenaire

My Family Tree
ISBN 0-7406-1008-2
ETA 351031

Revised American edition published in 2004 by ETA/Cuisenaire®
under license from Era Publications. All rights reserved.

ETA/Cuisenaire Product Development Manager: Mary Watanabe
Lead Editor: Betty Hey
Editorial Team: Kevin Anderson, Kim O'Brien, Nancy Sheldon,
  Elizabeth Sycamore
Educational Consultant: Geraldine Haggard, Ed.D.

ETA/Cuisenaire • Vernon Hills, IL 60061-1862
800-445-5985 • www.etacuisenaire.com

Printed in China.

04 05 06 07 08 09 10 11 12 13   10 9 8 7 6 5 4 3 2 1

Table of Contents

1 Getting Away

It was a Saturday afternoon, I remember, and I had just escaped to my tree. Down in the real world, I could hear the clatter of dish washing and the complaints of my younger brother, who hadn't been as quick as me. The street was quiet. The only signs of life were a spiral of smoke from the Bradys' grill across the road and our cat walking on the garage roof.

Then, it happened.

It started with a shout from my mother, who told me later she had seen him from the kitchen window as he fell over our back fence.

Then, I heard the sirens.

Then, I saw him. He was dressed in green and his face was very red. He jumped over the rose garden by our back door and came running down the side of our house, scattering some cardboard boxes and tripping over the firewood.

As he ran underneath me, he slowed down to regain his balance. Then, he made a mighty leap over our front fence, but only succeeded in catching his foot on our mailbox and tumbling onto the street. As he lay groaning in the gutter, I heard a screen door clatter and looked across to see Mr. Pescari from next door scurrying out to investigate. He doesn't usually miss much on our street, but he didn't see the man in green because he was too busy watching the first police car screeching around the corner with its siren blaring.

The man in green leaped to his feet with a cry of alarm, and Mr. Pescari leaped out of the way with a cry of terror. Two policemen leaped out of their car with a cry of triumph.

"There he is!" they shouted.

The chase was on again.

Mr. Pescari just stood there, mouth wide open like a circus clown, as the man in green sprinted back the way he had come. The man cleared our back fence on his first attempt and would have escaped if he hadn't run straight into Mrs. Easton's nightie, which was hanging on her clothesline.

I had to give evidence to the police because I was the only one who had seen everything. They told me the man had escaped from prison. When they untangled him from Mrs. Easton's nightie, he had a broken arm and gave up without a fight. Since that day, I've always thought that Mrs. Easton was tougher than she looked. But, that's because of the things I saw from up in my tree.

2 Neighborhood Watch

My tree was the place where I checked out the goings-on on our street. "Getting out of washing dishes," my younger brother called it. "Spying," my dad called it. My mom just called it the "neighborhood watch."

Ever since I could climb, I'd been going up my tree. And the bigger it grew, the higher I went and the more I discovered. Not that I saw Mrs. Easton catch an escaped prisoner with a nightie every day. But, as I climbed, the backyards and front yards opened up, and I started to see a different side to things.

Every morning, there was Mr. Cline taking his walk. Sometimes he would look up and see me and wave as he passed underneath. When I was on the ground, he seemed very tall. But, up in my tree, I noticed that his hair had thinned and he had a brown circle of skin like a little hat on the top of his head.

From my tree, I could watch Stefan next door grunting and kicking in the air as he practiced his karate. One day, I looked across and saw him in his karate clothes, standing motionless in front of a stack of roof tiles.

"ARRRGGGHHHH!"

His hand flashed down like a sword of steel and the clay tiles shattered. With Stefan as a neighbor, I was glad we had a shingle roof.

On the other side, of course, lived Mr. Pescari. Now, he had a real problem. My younger brother, who had spent his life acting stupid and giving people nicknames, called Mr. Pescari "Mr. Trampolini" because we could see him over the fence when we bounced on our trampoline. Mr. Pescari was from Sicily. "That's the football," my teacher told us, "right on the toe of Italy."

Mr. Pescari's real problem was my tree.

3 My Family Tree

My tree was planted for me outside my bedroom window by my Aunt Nina on the day I was born.

"A nice Norway maple tree. It will give you shade in the summer, and when the leaves fall in the winter, it won't block the sun," she would say to me. "And it will always remind you of where your mother, your grandparents, and I came from. It's your family tree."

When I first came home from the hospital, all I did was sleep and cry and eat (or so my Aunt Nina said). All my tree did was stand by Mr. Pescari's fence and slowly uncurl its leaves. It wasn't a problem for anyone.

But then, things started to happen.

"It's got its feet in the water at last," said Mr. Cline to my mother over the front fence as he walked past one morning. "You'll be able to climb to the top," he said to me, "and see the view very soon."

My mother gave him one of her dark looks, and I decided to learn to climb. Soon I could look into my bedroom, then I could peek over the fence, and then I started to discover the world.

Unfortunately for Mr. Pescari, that was when my tree became a part of his life, too. It grew quickly, too quickly for him, as it straggled up above the fence between our two yards. When the autumn wind blew, my tree dropped crinkly leaves in his yard and his gutters.

Mr. Pescari only grew plants that produced things to eat. He had a vegetable garden, three fruit trees, and a grapevine. And he only put up with the leaves dropping from his vine because it meant the next crop of grapes would soon be on their way.

Mr. Pescari sat on his porch and watched me in my tree. He raked the lawn and looked up at my tree. He dug in his garden and shook his head. He didn't like my tree at all.

"Tsk, tsk, tsk," he said to my dad every year, pointing to the overhanging branches. Then, my tree got a haircut and Mr. Pescari was quiet for a while.

"Why does he hate my tree so much?" I asked Dad.

"Well, for starters, Mr. Pescari probably thinks your tree deliberately drops its leaves on his side of the fence," he said. "And, it doesn't produce food like his garden. It just worries him."

"What's there to worry about?" I asked.

"When you were little, you worried, too. You wouldn't sleep in your room during a storm because the tree whistled in the wind and made scary shadows on the window. You thought it was someone out to get you."

"But, it doesn't worry me now."

"No, but it still worries Mr. Pescari. The more it spreads its branches toward his house, the darker the shadows are on his windows and the more he must think it's out to get him."

I still couldn't believe a tree would worry anyone as much as that.

As my tree grew up, I watched Mr. Pescari growing older. His hair went grayer and thinner, and he walked with a stoop even when he wasn't picking up leaves.

When I was twelve, my tree suddenly began to lose its leaves and not grow new ones. It began to creak and rustle, not sweep and swish. Its branches began bending like Mr. Pescari's back. We all knew something was wrong because twelve years isn't old for a tree.

"I think it's sick," said my dad.

"Doesn't look good," said Richard from up the road who works for a tree nursery.

Finally, I climbed to the top of my tree for the last time. I watched the color drain from the sky. Below me, I saw the glow of Mr. Pescari's television through the thinning branches. We sat and watched the news — me in my tree and Mr. Pescari in his living room.

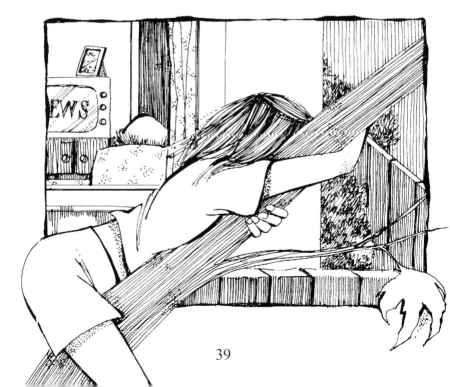

4 Forests or Fires?

Mr. Pescari helped cut down my tree. I played over at Yolanda's house and tried not to think about what was happening. When I came home, Mr. Pescari was humming a song as he sliced up the trunk into fire-sized pieces and stacked the neatest pile of firewood I had ever seen. He seemed to be taller. I had never seen him look so happy.

Without my tree, my window was now wide open to the sky. The morning sun flooded into my room and the toys on my bedside table twinkled. Without my tree, I played more basketball in the park and I rode down to the beach to go swimming. Mr. Pescari looked over the fence and almost smiled when he saw me come home.

5 Growing Up Again

On my thirteenth birthday, Mr. Pescari came and knocked on the door. He was very excited. He took us outside, and there in the spot where my tree used to be was a pot with a red ribbon around it. And in the pot was a small cherry tree with bright green leaves and little buds of fruit.

"An American tree, like us," he said, patting me on the shoulder. "Not like the tree with messy leaves."

"Thank you," I said, and Mr. Pescari did something that I had never seen before. He smiled so broadly, I suddenly realized he had gold fillings in his back teeth.

"Don't say anything!" I hissed to my younger brother who looked like he was just about to come up with a new nickname.

I have planted my tree now and it is growing well.

"It's got its feet in the water at last," says Mr. Cline to me over the front fence as he walks past. Mr. Pescari doesn't walk around much these days, but he likes to spend time sitting on his porch. He is keeping an eye on his share of the red fruit as the branches start to reach over the fence into his yard.